AQUARIUS

January 20–February 18

T0042831

Image by Andrea Lauren © Simon & Schuster, Inc.

✧ Susan B. Anthony ✧

Image by Andrea Lauren © Simon & Schuster, Inc.

Images by Andrea Lauren © Simon & Schuster, Inc., and 123RF/Volodymyr Horbovyy

ORCHID

Image by Andrea Lauren © Simon & Schuster, Inc.

Image by Andrea Lauren © Simon & Schuster, Inc.

Aquarius
I am
COMMITTED
to IMPROVING
the WORLD

Images by Andrea Lauren © Simon & Schuster, Inc., and 123RF/Volodymyr Horbovyy

Images by Andrea Lauren © Simon & Schuster, Inc., and 123RF/Volodymyr Horbovyy

Image by Andrea Lauren © Simon & Schuster, Inc.

winter

Image by Andrea Lauren © Simon & Schuster, Inc.

Aquarius

Image by Andrea Lauren © Simon & Schuster, Inc.

Aquarius
Ruled by Saturn and Uranus

Image by Andrea Lauren © Simon & Schuster, Inc.

Aquarius

Images by Andrea Lauren © Simon & Schuster, Inc., and 123RF/Volodymyr Horbovyy

Objective
INNOVATIVE
REBELLIOUS
INDEPENDENT
Friendly

Image by Andrea Lauren © Simon & Schuster, Inc.

Images by Andrea Lauren © Simon & Schuster, Inc., and 123RF/Volodymyr Horbovyy

Image by Andrea Lauren © Simon & Schuster, Inc.

RULING
HOUSE
11
The House of
Friendships

Image by Andrea Lauren © Simon & Schuster, Inc.

AQUARIUS

✧

I never give up on what I believe in

✧✧✧

Image by Andrea Lauren © Simon & Schuster, Inc.

Images © 123RF/Volodymyr Horbovyy and Getty Images/KavalenkavaVolha

Images by Andrea Lauren © Simon & Schuster, Inc., and 123RF/Volodymyr Horbovyy

Image by Andrea Lauren © Simon & Schuster, Inc.

AQUARIUS

Images © Getty Images/ElenaLux and 123RF/kotoffei

Aries
Taurus
Gemini
Cancer
Leo
Virgo
Libra
Scorpio
Sagittarius
Capricorn
Aquarius
Pisces

Images by Andrea Lauren © Simon & Schuster, Inc., and 123RF/Volodymyr Horbovyy

Air Signs
Aquarius
Libra
Gemini

Images by Andrea Lauren © Simon & Schuster, Inc., and 123RF/Volodymyr Horbovyy

LET THE STARS LEAD THE WAY

Image by Andrea Lauren © Simon & Schuster, Inc.